GARY JONES

Washington DC

First edition

This book was professionally typeset on Reedsy.
Find out more at reedsy.com

Contents

1

Introduction

Washington D.C. or simply "D.C." for many people is the capital of the United States of America. It is one of the most visited cities in the United States and around the world. Most of the federal government office, like the White House, Pentagon, and House of Congress, are found in the city. It also houses embassies from almost all the countries in the world.

The place is known for its scholarly history and reputation. It is filled with famous buildings, sites and other attractions dedicated to history and education. However, D.C. is more than just a scholarly place. It also offers the fun and excitement that other cities in the United States have.

D.C. has a lot to offer to local and international tourists. Many people claim that three days would not be enough to travel around the city. Three days is not even enough to travel the National Mall, which is only one of the attractions in the city.

Luckily, you have this book. It will help you plan a good three-day vacation in this wonderful city. It lists the top five good spots and attractions that you must visit and the best five places to eat, shop and stay. It also provides you with the directions on how to get to these places.

The book also provides the top things you should do while you are in the city. It also gives you strategies on how to enjoy some things in the city for free. Also, to keep you safe, the book provides you with tips on how to be safe in the city.

Enjoy this book and get ready to enjoy your three great days around D.C.

2

History of Washington D.C.

Washington D.C. was not the original capital of the United States of America. Many cities became the capital before it was legally declared to be the capital.

Before it was declared as the capital, the executive department and the Congress struggled to find a permanent capital. During the early 18th century, there was an ongoing conflict between the north and south region of the United States. The capital was often transferred to the region where the president came from.

In the late 18th century, President George Washington urged the Congress to declare a permanent location for the country's capital. The city was declared as Washington District of Columbia in 1800. The name was made in honor of President Washington, the named founder of the federal city. Despite the construction of the capital and vital federal government buildings, the city remained underdeveloped.

The city became the haven for runaway slaves during the early 19th century. It became the first city to have an African-American community. However, despite the increase of population, the economy of the city continued to go downhill.

During President Ulysses Grant's term in 1869, plans to modernize the city was brought to light. Sewers and necessary utilities were constructed in the city. However, the modernization bankrupted the city, leaving it unfinished and mostly in slump.

In 1901, the Congress decided to continue with the construction of the city. They relied again in L'Enfant original plan, which was to create beautiful boulevards, wide streets, and magnificent parks that could compete with those in Europe. New and modern neighborhoods were created around the city, eliminating the slums.

Other major federal government buildings, like the Pentagon, were constructed during the time of President Franklin Roosevelt. Over the years, the budget for the city increased every year as the city continued to be preserved and developed.

The City Tourism

Tourism Industry in the city was in mediocre since the creation of the city. In the 1970s, racism was rampant in the city. Local tourists rarely visited the city because of its large African-American communities.

The industry suffered more when the cocaine outbreak hit the city in the 1970's. The city became one of the most unsafe places in the country and a significant number of residents left.

It was only during the 1990's that the tourism industry recovered and grew because of the vast modernization introduced in the city.

Today, Washington DC is one of the top places to visit for international and local tourists. A trip to this historical city is a must when you visit the United States of America.

3

Overview of the City

The Downtown

The downtown is the center and the life of the city. Most of the top attractions in the city are found here. The National Mall, the White House, the largest public library in the country and the top museums are here.

The North Central

This area is famous among young adult tourists. The city has a bustling nightlife. There are plenty of trendy bars and restaurants that could keep the night alive.

The area is also known for being budget-friendly. Many hotels, restaurants and theaters can easily fit your budget. It is also under-an-hour away from the Downtown district. So, if you are in a tight budget, it is recommended that you find lodging in this area.

Embassies from many countries are also found in the North Central. Hence, you can meet many diverse tourists when strolling down this area.

The East

The east is rarely visited by tourists. It has the least to offer than the other three districts. Some parts of the area are still in slum. But, if you want to have a religious trip in Washington, it is the place to go.

The West

The district is home to the Georgetown University and the arguably wealthiest neighborhood in the city. You can find the houses of elites in this area. You cannot visit Washington without walking along the elite shopping strip in Chevy Chase.

4

When To Go

The DC Climate

The DC climate has a bad reputation because it can go to extremes. It can be too hot in the summer. However, it is not as bad as some claim them to be. The extremities of the weather add advantages and new things to do while in the city.

Spring is the most pleasant season for the city. It is filled with festivals and blooming flowers, including the famous cherry blossoms. At the beginning of spring, you can still experience low temperatures and rain. However, towards the end of the season, the weather becomes more suitable for walks around the parks.

Fall is also a pleasant season. The beginning of the fall is usually greeted with free concerts and festivals around the city. If the beauty of Spring is the blossoming flowers of cherry blossoms, the beauty of Fall is the changing of colors of the leaves. Many tourists enjoy a walk on the carroty-red streets along the National Mall and parks in the City.

As the season is about to change to winter, less people explore the city in the daytime. However, the streets become more festive as the city government prepares for its usual long winter holiday events. The city can be cold, but it is milder than most of the northern and southern states. Snow does not fall very often in the city, but the temperature drops relatively at night.

Summer is somehow the worst season in Washington. The summer sun is too hot and the air is too humid and dry. You can barely see locals walking around the city in the daytime and in weekends. Many of them would rather stay in their homes to cool down than roam around the city. Some locals would also go out of the city to enjoy the good beaches from the adjacent cities.

The Best Time to Visit

Spring

Most local would tell you to visit in spring. The weather is perfect. The city is blooming. Festivals, free shows and other activities are lined up. You can also have a great view of the city while the blooming cherry blossoms decorate it.

However, the best time for the locals may not be the best time for you. It all depends on your budget and the time you have to spare in the city. Since this book is about traveling around DC in three days, spring may not be the best time to visit.

Many tourists, local and international, flock the city during spring. Many educational tours are hosted during this season. The museums and other attractions would be crowded with many students from around the world. You would have less quiet moments and less photo opportunity. You will also have a limited time to roam around the National Mall because it can get too crowded. Most restaurants and bars would also be crowded.

The prices shoot up during this season, too. Hotel rates are about thirty percent higher than they were during winter. Entrances to other attractions are also increased to control the influx of tourists. Prices of local delicacies and souvenirs are also higher than the usual.

Fall

This season is best for short trips. It offers almost the same things as Spring, except for the exquisite view of blooming cherry blossoms. However, if you come at around mid-September to mid-October, you can witness the changing of colors of trees around the National Mall and nearby parks.

There are many festivals in fall, too. Come in the last week of August or first week of September to catch free concerts for returning college students.

The National Mall and other top tourist spots would still be crowded, but not as much as spring or summer. You can still travel around the city in comfort and with fewer crowds.

Winter

It may not be the best season to come, but it has its own beauty. Three days would be enough to travel all the top spots and attractions around the city during winter. The museums and other historical spots are almost empty. You can roam around the museums as much as you want. You can read the descriptions without having to wait or push the person before you.

Hotel prices may be lower by about ten percent than fall and thirty percent than spring. Shopping malls would offer early Christmas shopping events in December. Pedicab fees, theater tickets, touring bus fees and private museums tickets also drop. Thus, you can get good value for your money.

Summer

It is probably the worst time to get a vacation in DC, but it can be a good time for a three-day trip, especially at dates near July 4 or the Independence Day. However, expect that hotels and nearby lodging houses would be packed by tourists. Also, expect that the rates of almost everything would go up.

There would be sponsored Independence Day concerts and activities around the city. There will also be an annual fireworks festival, which is best seen in high buildings with a full view of the city.

The rest of the summer can be quite challenging for tourists, especially if you are not accustomed to the hot weather. The National Mall and the usual tourist spots would not be crowded, but you may not have the strength to travel around for a whole day because of the temperature.

5

Getting to and Getting By

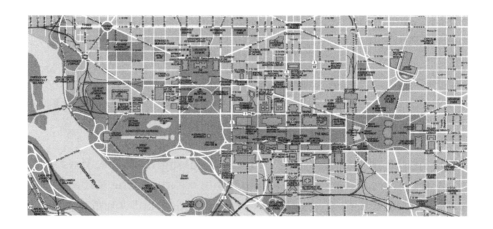

Getting to Washington DC

By Air

Ronald Raegan National Airport

2401 S Smith Boulevard, Arlington, Virginia
+1 703-417-8000

Ronald Raegan National Airport Website
www.flyreagan.com
Ronald Raegan National Airport Map
https://goo.gl/maps/VnUDFuDknPn

This airport is named after the 40th president of the United States, Ronald Reagan. It is the nearest airport to downtown DC. It is also near residence area, which is the reason for its limited flight.

Not everyone can enter or leave through the airport. It has no custom clearing facilities. Hence, there are only limited international flights received. Only flights from countries of origin that has custom pre-clearance system, like Canada, may be accepted in the airport.

The airport does not only service flights, but it also has extra services. It offers meeting space rental, so you can have your business meetings directly at the airport, upon your arrival. It also has exhibit halls that show the history of the airport.

You can also shop and dine in the airport upon arrival or before departure. A strip of shops and restaurants are available in the hall that connects the terminals. There are convenience stores, pet shops and even spa.

There are four ways to leave the airport. You can leave by Metrorail, taxi, bus and rental cars.

Metrorail station, operated by WMATA, can service you to the Downtown and the East End stations. The fare price to these stations is around $3 to $5.

Metro Bus only operates in the weekend or after the Metrorail station service hours has ended. Though it is slower than the Metrorail, you can take the opportunity to sightsee the town. The basic fare for the bus is around $2 to $4, depending on the peak and off-peak hours.

You can take a taxi from the airport or rideshare by Uber and Lyft. A trip to the Downtown or East End may cost you around $10 to $15, depending on the traffic.

You can also rent a car. There are booths for car rentals in the airport. You can rent them if you have all the necessary documents with you. However, most of them only prefer pre-booked rental.

Metrorail Website

https://www.wmata.com/service/rail/
Phone:202-637-7000

Washington Dulles International Airport

1 Saarinen Cir, Dulles, Virginia
+1 703-572-2700

Washington Dulles International Airport Website
www.mwaa.com
Washington Dulles International Airport Map
https://goo.gl/maps/DWXFrdLApCv

Washington Dulles International Airport is the primary international airport in the city. It is complete with international flight services and serves almost all international airlines from around the world.

It is significantly far from the Downtown DC. It takes about two hours to reach the Downtown via Metrorail. Also, the terminals are not connected. You may have to travel using the on-airport bus service

GETTING TO AND GETTING BY

or trains to get from the ticketing office to your terminal.

How to get to Downtown DC

There is no direct Metrorail station that connects the airport to Downtown or any end of the city. You need to ride buses to get to the nearest Metrorail station. There are two buses that operate from the airport. These are Silver Line Express Bus and Metro Bus.

The cheapest way to get to DC is through the Super Shuttle and Supreme Airport Shuttle. The basic fee is $30 for the first person and $10 for the succeeding persons. It can bring you directly to the East End of DC. The travel time would be around 60 to 80 minutes.

Another cheap way to get to the Downtown is by Uber transport pooling. The fee to Downtown DC would be around $35. The advantage of using Uber pooling is that they will bring you to your hotel or your destination instead of dropping you to the nearest stop.

Another way to get to the Downtown directly is by the Washington Flyer Taxi. It is the exclusive taxi service in the airport. It is safe and reliable. The fare is around $75.

You can also rent a car from the airport. However, most of the car rental company requires pre-booking. So, if you want to drive your way to DC, you should make the preparations prior to your arrival.

Baltimore-Washington International Thurgood Marshall Airport

Baltimore, Maryland
+1 410-859-7111

Baltimore-Washington International Thurgood Marshall Airport

Website

https://www.bwiairport.com/

Baltimore-Washington International Thurgood Marshall Airport Map

https://goo.gl/maps/1SevuysqTmL2

Baltimore-Washington International Thurgood Marshall Airport is the only airport to DC that serves from the state of Maryland. It is also the farthest to the Downtown DC, being 30 miles away from the city. It takes around 2 hours to travel from the airport to the Downtown through the Metrorail.

Among the three servicing airports to DC, it is considered to have the best service and amenities. It has shops, restaurants, spas, and fitness center. It is also children friendly. It has nursing rooms and playhouses for children.

Getting to Downtown DC

It is a little difficult to use public transport from the airport. It requires many transfers from one bus to another before you can reach the nearest Metrorail station. The nearest station from the airport is the BWI Rail Station. The nearest station to East End is the Union Station, where you can catch the bus to go to Downtown and other destination.

Super Shuttle is still the cheapest way to get to Downtown DC. The basic rate for the first passenger is $42. The bus leaves at exactly 20 minutes after the first ticket for the bus was sold.

Uber pooling is another option in BWI airport. The basic fare is around $50. If you take the Uber taxi service, the fee would be around $80 to $110.

Taxi service is offered from the airport, too. The fare to Downtown

DC reaches from $100 to $130.

You can also opt for car rentals from any of the car rental companies available in the airport.

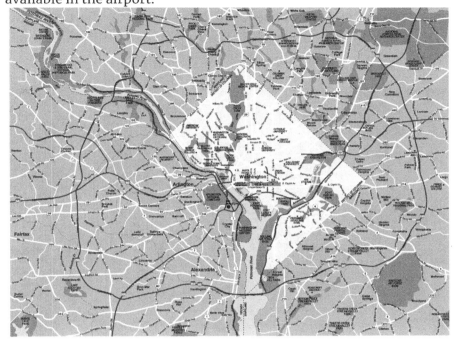

By Land

Trains

Amtrak trains to the city are available from any major cities in the United States. They all stop at the Union Station, which is about twenty minutes away from the Downtown station.

To get to the Downtown, you can transfer directly to a Metrorail red.

Get off to the Farragut North Station and you will be walking distance away from the major spots in Downtown. It would take around 10 to 15 minutes to reach Downtown.

You can also take the Metrobus to the Downtown. There are buses that serve from the station to the Downtown. A bus trip takes around 20 to 30 minutes, depending on the traffic.

The Union Station is also near the National Mall. From the Union Station, you can get off from the Metro Center Station and walk your way to the National Mall.

Union Station Washington DC Website
https://www.unionstationdc.com/
Union Station Washington DC Map

https://goo.gl/maps/Mxhcs8qUPW12

By Car

You can also reach the city through a road trip from anywhere in the United States. However, if you are only staying in DC for three days, driving to the city is not advisable because of the traffic during peak hours.

By Bus

You can also ride the bus to the city from any city in the country, especially if you are in New York. There are many bus companies that service a ride from New York City to the Union Station in DC.

Some tourists from Boston or nearby towns have more chances of getting a direct bus ride from New York to the city. You can choose from regular buses to luxury buses, depending on your budget.

Getting Around the City

Understanding the Layout

The City is divided in four quadrants. The division is different from the districts as mentioned in the previous chapter. The quadrants will help you plan better on how to go around the city in three days.

The center of the city is the United States Capitol Building. The capitol is about a mile away from the Union Station. From the Capitol, draw perpendicular lines to create the quadrant. Now, you will have the northwest, northeast, southeast and southwest of the city.

You need to understand this because some instructions in this book and even by the locals will only refer to this quadrant when helping you how to get to the place you want to go. Also, all the addresses would always include the quadrant for easy location.

Most of the top tourist spots are usually found in the northwest of the city. The Northwest have the biggest area among the quadrants.

Once you cross the opposite side of the National Mall, you would find yourself in the southwest area, which is also the smallest area for tourists. Most of the southwest region is covered by Pentagon and other military facilities.

The Northeast of the city is the second largest area, but it is more of a residential area, just like the Southeast region of the city.

The Best Way to Go Around

Walking

Walking is the best way to go around DC, especially if you are around the Northwest quadrant of the city. All the top tourist spots in the city are less than a mile away from each other that you can easily walk from one location to the other.

The more you walk in DC, the more you get to see the hidden sites and hidden shops that you cannot find when riding a car or any public transport. Thus, packing a good pair of sneakers for your vacation is highly recommended.

Bicycle

Another good way to travel around the city is by bicycle. It is almost efficient as walking, but you cannot just stop at anywhere you want to. Some shops and restaurants do not have parking spaces for bicycle. You need to park your bicycle in specific areas, which could sometimes be a little far from the attraction you want to see.

You do not have to pack your own bicycle. There are hundreds stations of bicycle rentals around the city. It is easy to rent, too. The packages for bicycle rental ranges from $2 to $10, depending on the length of time you want to use it.

Below are some of the companies that service bicycle rentals around the city:

Capital Bikeshare

Capital Bikeshare Website

www.capitalbikeshare.com
Capital Bikeshare Map
https://goo.gl/maps/pwmUxowveCu
Phone:1-877-430-2453

This is the leading bike shop rental in the city. It has over 100 stations. All transactions are done electronically. You register with them through their website, choose and pay the rental pass you want. After becoming a member, you can go to the nearest Capital Bikeshare station and unlock a bike using your pin.

Every ride should be under thirty minutes to avoid extra charges. You should check in to another station every thirty minutes to stop the time meter from running. You only need to lock in the bike to the station. Make sure that the light turns green before you leave. The green light signals that the bike is safely locked. After you locked the bike, you can again unlock it if you have an unlimited pass package.

Bike-Station

Bike-Station Website
www.bikestation.com
Bike-Station Map

https://goo.gl/maps/GWacLSvQXJR2
Phone:+1 202-962-0206
50 Massachusetts Ave NE, Washington

Bike Station has many stations around the city. It does not work like the Capital Bikeshare. You have to go to their shop to rent a bike. They also have limited bicycle for rent because it is not their main business. Bikestation is a shop where you can leave your bike while you work or explore around the area. It also serves as a repair shop for bikes.

You have to become a member through their website or by visiting their stations. Choose from the packages they offer for bike rentals and use the bike around the city. You can ride the bike without any time limit.

However, if you lose the bike, you will have to pay for it. If you have to park the bike, you should be equipped with your own lock or park it in the nearest Bike-Station location in the city, which is not as many as the other bike-share company.

Pedicab

Pedicab Website
http://www.dcpedicab.com/en

Pedicab Map
https://goo.gl/maps/iFHPhneqEY12

A pedicab is a bike with a backseat. It works like a rickshaw or a coach, but only driven with a bicycle. It is a popular way of getting around in the city because riding it is also an experience.

It is common around the National Mall area. You can opt to engage the service of a pedicab to get to the places of your choice or you can get a pedicab tour offered by some pedicab companies.

Below are some of the pedicab companies that service around the city:
DC Pedicab

1300 Pennsylvania Avenue NW
+1 202-345-8065

DC Pedicab Website
www.dcpedicab.com

DC Pedicab units can hold three persons and two children below four years old. Their units are spacious enough to carry some of your big luggage or purses. It is also stable and does not wobble even if the driver is making a turn.

It does not operate as a taxi on bike. You cannot ride it by demand. You have to get a reservation with them before you can ride. They offer sightseeing tour packages, which allow you to travel around the top tourist spots in the northwest area. Sightseeing tours cost around $85 to $95 per hour and depending on the number of passengers.

If you want to make your own tour and only use the service for getting around, you can book a reservation with the company. You can contact them by phone or their website for the prices. The basic fee is the same as the sightseeing tours, but additional fees are added when you travel outside of the usual route.

The pedicabs from this company are often in color yellow.

Capitol Pedicabs

+1 202 232-6086
Capitol Pedicabs Website
www.capitalpedicab.com
Capitol Pedicabs Map
https://goo.gl/maps/tSgNHP8yzjB2

Capitol Pedicabs is the leading company in pedicab service in Washington DC. Its charges start at around $60. It can house about three adults or two adults with 2 children below five years old.

You can take the pedicab from the National Mall to Georgetown Mall or vice versa. You can avail of their pedicab tours or you can create your own itinerary. The price is still around $60 per hour, provided that your destination is along the two aforesaid malls.

You can also engage the services of the pedicabs as your personal service. You can book a pedicab for the whole day. The driver would act like your chauffeur and you can take the pedicab anywhere in the city.

The company's pedicabs are usually in white color.

Non-partisan Pedicabs

1100 Pennsylvania Avenue Northwest Washington
+1 707 231-9882

Non-partisan Pedicabs Website
www.nonpartisanpedicab.com
Non-partisan Pedicabs Map
https://goo.gl/maps/udYF4uXZt3M2

Non-partisan Pedicabs operate like a personal tour guide and a chauffeur at the same time. Unlike the first two companies, they only service specific tours. The tours can take about an hour to three hours.

They also charge by passenger. One passenger is around $45 per hour. They only allow two adult passengers in a pedicab and one child below seven years old. Two children are considered as one adult.

While on tour, you can ask the chauffeur to bring you to shops, restaurants or café that is within the area of the tour.

Their pedicabs are usually painted yellow with vivid black upholstery.

National Pedicabs

+1 202-269-9090

National Pedicabs Website
www.nationalpedicabs.com
National Pedicabs Map
https://goo.gl/maps/dqPpcrvssSD2

National pedicabs work as taxis. You can get them on-demand or by reservation. You can call them when you arrive in the city and they will be at your service at the rate of $75 per hour. The pedicab can take three adults or four children.

You can also enjoy some of their tours or make your own tour around the city. One of the charms of this company is their funny drivers. The drivers sometimes dressed in costumes and entertain you as you take a tour around the city.

Their pedicabs are usually colored green.

Buses

Most of the bus stops are near the attractions around the city, so you can minimize your walking time. The fare usually starts at $1 to $10 depending on your point of origin and destination.

Riding the bus is not advisable during peak hours. You can get stuck in traffic for hours. However, if you only want to go for a quick sight-seeing around town, riding the bus can be a good way.

There are three buses that operate in the city. These are:

Metrobus

The company services almost all routes around the city. You can get to almost any avenue or street in the city through the bus. However, the buses are not tourist friendly. They are operating as a public transport just as how a public transport should operate.

Metrobus Website
https://www.wmata.com/service/bus/
Metrobus Map
https://goo.gl/maps/WGGF6aCAvf42

DC Circulator Buses

These buses are visitor friendly. They offer routes that double as a tour near the attractions and some neighborhood in the city. The fare is around $1 for every route. Discounts are given to senior citizens. Also, if you transferred from a Metrobus or Metrorail from the Union Station, the first route is often free.

DC Circulator Buses Website

http://www.dccirculator.com/
Phone:202-671-2020

Taxis and Rideshare

Taxis and rideshare are also good ways to travel around the city, but they can also be the most expensive next to the pedicab. Uber and Lyft operate in the city and you can contact them by downloading their apps in your smartphone.

As for taxis, there are many companies that offer their services. Since it is prohibited for a taxi to serve outside its route, some of the companies may not be able to serve you from or to the airports.

Yellow Cab

+1 202 544-1212 or +1 202 TAXICAB

It is the largest taxi company operating in the city. Their services are tested and proven. Like all taxi companies, it accepts credit cards as payment. The taxis from these companies are allowed to fetch or bring you to the airports outside the city.

DC Taxi Service

1 202-276-4976

It is a company that exclusively operates in DC. It also accepts credit cards as payment. Some of their units are not allowed to operate outside the city. Thus, it cannot bring or fetch you from the airports.

By Car

It may be convenient to drive by car because you can go to the place you want to go at any time you want. However, using a rented car can be expensive because of the parking fees around the town. You cannot park your car in one spot for more than two hours or you will be charged with parking fees. You might end up spending $30 to $50 to parking fees alone.

If you want to drive around the city on your own, you can rent your car from some of the car rental companies listed below:

Enterprise Rent a Car

Enterprise Rent A Car is a leading rent-a-car company in the US. They have branches around the city. You can choose and pick up a car in their shop. You may also rent the car online and they would deliver the car to you. The rent varies depending on the type of vehicle and the length of the rent.

Enterprise Rent a Car Website
www.enterprise.com

The shops are open only from 9:00a.m. to 6:00 p.m.

Avis Rent a Car

Avis is a worldwide rent a car company. They have shops in all the point of entry to Washington DC and a few more around the city. You can rent a car from the airport or the Union Station directly. You may also register and make a reservation through their website.

Avis Rent a Car Website
www.avis.com

The shops in the airport operate 24 hours, whereas the others open at 7:00a.m. and closes at 7:00p.m. The rate varies to the type of vehicle and the period of rent. Prices may also change depending on the season.

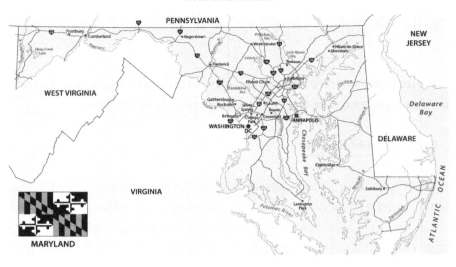

6

Where to Stay

Washington can be an expensive place to stay, but there are many hotels that can still fit your budget and still give you comfort while you are enjoying the city. Below are the top five comfortable and affordable hotels around the city:

The Westin Washington

1400 M St. NW, Washington, DC 20005, USA
+1 202-429-1700
The Westin Washington Website
http://www.starwoodhotels.com/westin/
The Westin Washington Map
https://goo.gl/maps/5rEquHtdX132

The hotel is only 2 minutes away from the White House and about ten minutes away from the National Mall. It is located at the heart of Northwest. It is near many restaurants, bar and shops.

Amenities include: Parking (with fee), free Wi-Fi, in-house bar, complimentary breakfast, indoor fitness center, concierge services, ATM

Room Facilities: Air conditioning and heating, flat screen television with cable channels, desk, coffee makers, bathroom (shower or bath), telephone, fridge, hairdryer, and free toiletries.

If you have pets, you can ask for pet beds or necessary pet facilities from the lobby.

Rooms available: Traditional room with single king bed, traditional family room, city view room with single king bed, city view family room, and studio suits.

Price range: $100 to $380, depending on the room and number of guest.

Check in & out times: 3:00pm and 12:00pm

How to get there from the Union Station: The fastest way is through the metro rail.

Take the red metro line and board the train to Farragut Square Station. From there, walk towards Connecticut Avenue and proceed to L Street. Turn left to 16th Street and walk to M street. You can easily find the hotel from there.

Embassy Row Hotel

2015 Massachusetts Ave. NW, Washington, DC 20036, USA
+1 202-265-1600
Embassy Row Hotel Website
www.destinationhotels.com
Embassy Row Hotel Map
https://goo.gl/maps/eBMa2AuKj5S2

The hotel is located a few miles away from DuPont Circle, which is considered as the center of NorthWest, Washington, DC. It is surrounded by many embassies from around the world. It is also near many restaurants of different cuisines. It is also near the National Zoo and about twenty minutes away from Georgetown University and the National Mall. It is also near bustling live music bars.

Amenities include: Parking (with fee), free Wi-Fi, rooftop lounge and swimming pools, indoor fitness center, concierge services, ATM, complimentary breakfast, daily maid services, on-site coffee house and snack bar, restaurant and bar and game rooms.

Room Facilities: Air conditioning and heating, flat screen television with cable channels, radio and iPod dock, wide desk, coffee makers, bathroom (shower or bath), telephone, fridge, hairdryer, and free toiletries.

If you have pets, you can ask for pet beds or necessary pet facilities from the lobby.

Rooms available: Deluxe room, double deluxe room, City view deluxe room, City view double deluxe room, SOME suites. Extra beds are available and charge around $20.

Price range: $90 to $400, depending on the room and number of guest.

Check in & out times: 3:00pm and 12:00pm

How to get there from the Union Station: The best way to reach the hotel from the Union Station is by bus.

Walk to North Capitol Street and E Street station. Board the bus heading west to Sibley Hospital in the Northwest. There would be 18 stops before you reach the stop near the hotel. Get off at 20th Street and N Street bus stop. From there, walk further to P Street. Turn to Massachusetts Avenue and head to the hotel.

Hamilton Hotel

1001 14th St., Northwest
+1 202-682-0111
Hamilton Hotel Website
www.hamiltonhoteldc.com
Hamilton Hotel Map
https://goo.gl/maps/qmf3bES86Du

If you plan to take a lot of cultural visit in the city, this hotel is highly recommended. It is seated at the heart of the city for tourists. The National Mall is only a few minute-walk from the hotel. It is also in walking distance to the nearest metro rail station. Among the hotels near the National Mall, it is one with the most competitive room prices, too.

Amenities include: Parking (with fee), free Wi-Fi, vending machines, on-site Star Bucks, on-site restaurant and snack bar, breakfast delivery, concierge service, laundry service, maid service, ATM and interpreter service for 10 languages, special diet services, fitness, and spa.

Room Facilities: Air conditioning and heating, flat screen television with cable and satellite channels, radio, cd player and iPod dock, wide desk, telephone, iron, coffee/tea makers, bathroom (shower or bath), bathrobes, and free toiletries.

If you have pets, you can ask for pet beds or necessary pet facilities from the lobby.

All rooms are sound-proofed.

Rooms available: single room, double room, king room, queens room, executive suite, junior suite

Price range: $75 to $250, depending on the room and number of guest. Charges may increase when nearing Independence Day and Cherry Blossom Festival.

Check in & out times: 3:00pm and 12:00pm

How to get there from the Union Station: The best way to reach the hotel from the Union Station is by bus.

Walk to North Capitol Street and Massachusetts Avenue. Board the bus heading South of Kennedy Center. There would be 12 stops before you reach the stop near the hotel. Get off at 14th Street and K Street bus stop. Move east to 14th street until you reach the hotel.

High Road Hostel

1804 Belmont Rd NW, Washington
+1 202-735-3622
High Road Hostel Website
http://highroadhostels.com/
High Road Hostel Map
https://goo.gl/maps/QiWJMMbSwUB2

You can still stay in a comfortable way in Washington, DC even with a tight budget. All thanks to the High Road Hostel. It is only about 3 kilometers away from the National Mall and less than a mile from DuPont Circle. You can enjoy good restaurants and bars around the area and explore the nightlife.

It may not be as exquisite as the hotel, but it will give you a comfortable stay while you are in DC. It also prides itself with the best Wi-Fi connection for their guests.

The hostel does not accept children and pets. Also, there are no elevators or lifts.

Amenities include: Parking (with fee), free Wi-Fi, maid services, ironing service, vending machines, locker rentals, shared kitchen and lounge area, gaming area and TV viewing, contemporary breakfast.

Room Facilities: Air conditioning and heating, shared bathroom for dorm rooms (shower), hairdryer, and free toiletries

Rooms available: 4-bed dormitory room, 6-bed dormitory room, 14-bed backpacker's room, 8-bed backpacker's room, group rooms (2 or 4 rooms exclusive for travelers in groups).

Price range: $20 to $40 per person in shared rooms, $120 to $140 for the group rooms.

Check in & out times: 4:00pm and 11:00pm

How to get there from the Union Station: The best way to reach the hostel from the Union Station is by bus.

Walk to Massachusetts Avenue and First Street Bus Stop. Board the bus heading west to Duke Ellington Bridge. There would be 21 stops before you reach the stop near the hotel. Get off at 18th Street and Belmont Road bus stop. Follow Belmont Road and you can find the hostel.

Days Inn Washington DC

4400 Connecticut Avenue Northwest, Northwest
+1 202-244-5600
Days Inn Washington DC Website
www.wyndhamhotels.com
Days Inn Washington DC Map
https://goo.gl/maps/R1m2dH4hayo

The hotel is about 10km away from the National Mall, 3km away from the DuPont Circle, but less than a mile away from the National Zoo and other famous parks around the city. It is a simple hotel that can provide comfort to your family when you visit DC. It has competitive room prices that could even compete with hostels in the city.

However, the hotel is not pet-friendly.

Amenities include: Parking (with fee), free Wi-Fi, vending machines, on-site car rental, on-site restaurant and bar, gift shop, priority access to a nearby golf course, daily maid services, and dry cleaning services (with fee).

Room Facilities: Air conditioning and heating, private bathroom, free toiletries, hairdryer, flat screen television with cable channels, radio, telephone, iron, and coffee maker, desk.

Rooms available: Double Deluxe Room, Kings Room, Queens Room, Double Room, Business Kings Room

Price range: $45 to $140, depending on the number of guests
Check in & out times: 3:00pm and 11:00pm

How to get there from the Union Station: The best way to reach the hotel is by Metrorail.

Board the red line through Shady Grove. You will get off at the 8th stop, which is the Van Ness UDC Station. From there, head northwest to Connecticut Avenue until you find the hotel on the left side of the road.

7

Top Five Restaurants to Visit

Top Five Restaurants to Visit

Ambar Restaurant in Capitol Hill

523 8th St, Southeast
+1 202-813-3039
Ambar Restaurant Website
www.ambarrestaurant.com
Ambar Restaurant Map
https://goo.gl/maps/Uc7n7QHYVkz

This restaurant is a 20-minute walk from the U.S. Capitol and a 20-minute ride from the National Mall. It is a European style restaurant which is the usual destination for tourists after a tour in the National Mall. It offers vegetarian, vegan, gluten-free and other allergy-free menus. Just ask the restaurant captain or server and they will present you with a different menu. Most of the dishes are not child-friendly.

Cuisine: Balkan

Famous Menu: Balkan Salad, Mimosa, mezze of different meats, bread with Balkan spreads, open-faced sandwiches, Vienna Schnitzel, kebabs and drunken mussels.

What sets it apart: Aside from the fact that it is perhaps the only few Balkan restaurant in the State, it also offers a different dining experience. The seats on one side of the restaurants are continuous, which can be great for big groups.

The restaurant also offers the $49 experience. It is an offer of unlimited small plates and selected drinks per person. However, everyone in the table should choose the same option.

Prices: Average price for a dish is around $7, Chef's plate is around $19, and meat mezze is at $20. You can also try their horizontal and vertical tasting of drinks for $21.

Service time: Brunch is available only on weekends from 10:00am to 3:30 pm. Lunch is served from 11:00am to 2:00pm. Dinner is served from 4:00pm to 10:00pm (11:00pm on Fridays and Saturdays).

How to get there from the National Mall: The easiest way to get to the restaurant is by the Metrorail.

Board the Metrorail heading southeast from the Federal Triangle Station or Smithsonian Station. Get off at the Eastern Market Station. Head to Pennsylvania Avenue and turn right on 8th Street.

Annie's Paramount Steakhouse

609 17th St Northwest
+1 202-232-0395
Annie's Paramount Steakhouse Website
www.annies.biz

Annie's Paramount Steakhouse Map
https://goo.gl/maps/UM6nYRL28e92

The steakhouse is located near DuPont Circle. It is near many of the hotels around the area. It is also about 10 minutes away from the White House and 20 minutes away from the National Mall.

Cuisine: American

Famous Menu: prime rib steak, southern fried chicken, burgers, "bull in a pan"

What sets it apart: The restaurant prides itself with their friendly and lively atmosphere. It is a longtime favorite restaurant for the city locals because the menus are affordable and delicious. The servings are also generous. Some locals even call it an affordable five-star steakhouse.

Prices: Average price for burgers and sandwiches is around $11.

Steaks range from $18 to $49. Other dishes range from $11 to $49.

Service time: Monday to Thursday, 11:00am to 10:00pm; Friday and

Saturday, 11:00am to 11:00pm; Sunday: 9:00am to 10:00pm.

How to get there from the National Mall: The fastest way is riding a bus heading to Silver Spring station near DuPont Circle. The bus stop is located at 12th Street and Constitution Avenue. Get off at 16th Street and Q Street stop. Head to 17th Street to find the restaurant.

Old Ebbit Restaurant

675 15th St NW, Washington, DC 20005, USA
+1 202-347-4800
Old Ebbit Restaurant Website
www.ebbitt.com
Old Ebbit Restaurant Map
https://goo.gl/maps/NbbnCJHZBp22

This restaurant is one of the oldest restaurants in DC. It began operating in 1856, but only moved to its current location in 1983. Many famous politicians and persons had eaten in this restaurant. It is only less than half a mile away from the White House.
Cuisine: American

Famous Menu: oyster, crab cakes, burgers and fries, eggs benedict, grilled steaks and fishes, farmhouse cheese platter

What sets it apart: The restaurant has history and considered as a historic landmark by the locals.

Prices: Soups are at around $6. Other dishes are priced from $10 to $25.
Service time: The restaurant is open from 7:00am to 2:00am during weekdays and 8:30am to 2:00am on weekends.

How to get there from the National Mall: The fastest way to get there is through the Metrorail. Board the train in Federal Triangle or Smithsonian Station and head northwest to Metro Center Station. Head west to 13th Street and turn left to 15th Street to find the restaurant.

&Pizza

1005 E St NW, Washington, DC 20004, USA

+1 202-347-5056
&Pizza Website
www.andpizza.com
&Pizza Map
https://goo.gl/maps/mBFpkT7wab72

Considered as the number one pizza house in the city, &Pizza are proud to serve tourists and locals with their gourmet pizzas. It has many branches around the city, but the most popular one is the one near the White House and the National Mall.

Cuisine: Comfort Food, Italian

Famous Menu: Maverick Pizza, Unlimited Topping Pizza, Moonstruck Pizza

What sets it apart: It is a simple pizza house that allows you to create your own pizza according to your preference. It also gives you the chance to experience cooking your own pizzas. It is child-friendly, vegetarian and vegan-friendly.

Prices: Soups are at $6. Other dishes are priced from $10 to $25.

Service time: The restaurant is open from 11:00am to 11:00pm from Sunday to Thursday and 11:00am to 12:00pm on Friday and Saturday.

How to get there from the National Mall: The location is less than half a mile away from the National Mall. You can walk or bike from the Smithsonian Metrorail Station and head north to 12th Street. Turn right to E street and you can find the quaint pizza shop.

The Crimson Diner

627 H St NorthWest

+1 202-847-4454

The Crimson Diner Website

www.crimson-dc.com

The Crimson Diner Map

https://goo.gl/maps/nLC9SBmmUER2

The diner is seated in the heart of the Chinatown in Washington. It is relatively new, but it is getting attention from both tourists and locales. It is a 20-minute walk from the National Mall and less than a five-minute walk from the Capital One Arena, home of the Washington Wizards.

Cuisine: Comfort Food, American

Famous Menu: fried chicken burger, devil eggs, crimson burger, hush puppies and fried green tomatoes

What sets it apart: It has a classy design like an authentic American diner, in taste and in price. It offers new menu that are not usually found in regular diners. Customers are curious about their pink devil eggs. The restaurant also operates a whiskey bar and a seasonal rooftop bar.

Prices: The price range is around $11 to $30.

Service time: The restaurant is open from 7:00am to 12:00am from Sunday to Thursday and 7:00am to 1:00am on Friday and Saturday.

How to get there from the National Mall: You can go North by following 7th Street. When you reach H Street, turn right. The restaurant is around the corner.

8

Top Five Bars and Pubs to Visit

Top Five Bars and Pubs to Visit

Penn Social Bar

801 E St NW, Washington, DC 20004, USA
+1 202-697-4900
Penn Social Bar Website
www.pennsocialdc.com
Penn Social Bar Map
https://goo.gl/maps/q9qVgS15dnw

Penn Social is a place to socialize with friends or to meet new acquaintances. The place is filled with games, from football to board games. It has three bars and a patio.

Local bands play every Friday. The Trivia game is launched every Tuesday. You can watch NFL, NBA, NCAA and other Sports events from televisions strategically placed around the bar.

It serves famous beers and cider. It also has a wide array of local draft beers. You can have tacos, quesadilla, chicken poppers and more to accompany your beer.

The bar stays open from 4:00pm to 12:00am on weekdays. It opens at noon on Saturday and closes at 3:00am. On Sunday, it opens at noon and closes at midnight.

Price: for drinks the average is $7/glass and $28/pitcher; for finger foods, the average is $12.

How to get there from the National Mall: Head north of 9th Street until you reach E Street. Turn right and the bar would be at the corner.

McClellan's Retreat

2031 Florida Ave Northwest

+1 202-265-6270
McClellan's Retreat Website
www.mcclellansretreat.com
McClellan's Retreat Map
https://goo.gl/maps/g3CshhgP7tT2

It is situated just a few meters from Embassy Row Hotel. It is a bit peaceful compared to the regular bars in the area. You can come here to unwind and relax after a day of roaming around the city.

It offers special drinks depending on the occasion, but they also have their usual drinks. The most famous drinks are McClellan Manhattan and Pepperbox. You can also choose the snack menu of your choice, such as cheese plates and a variety of fried foods.

Price: For the drinks, the price starts at $8 while the price starts at $11 for the snacks.

How to get there from the National Mall: Head to the Constitution Avenue Station and ride the Metrorail heading to the DuPont Circle Station. Get off and head to Q Street to the east of the station. Turn left on Connecticut Avenue and take another left to Florida Avenue.

Pearl Street Warehouse

33 Pearl Street Southwest
+1 202-380-9620
Pearl Street Warehouse Website
www.pearlstreetwarehouse.com
Pearl Street Warehouse Map
https://goo.gl/maps/vgUKqdmyv5A2

Pearl Street is a new music bar in Washington, but it quickly became one of the top bars in the city. If you are a music lover and want to enjoy good music near the waterfront, head down to the south and have a drink at this warehouse. It is open from 7:30 am till midnight. It serves breakfast, lunch and dinner. All meals are accompanied with good music.

Prices: Prices for both food and drinks starts at $5.

How to get there from the National Mall: Board the Metrorail from the Federal Triangle Station or Smithsonian Station heading to L'Enfente Plaza Station. From the station, walk towards D Street.

Make a left to 7th Street SW and another right to the junction of Pearl and Water Streets.

Penn Quarter Sports Bar

639 Indiana Ave Northwest
+1 202-347-6666
Penn Quarter Sports Bar Website
www.pennquartersportstavern.com
Penn Quarter Sports Bar Map
https://goo.gl/maps/KE3GwmZvn852

Tourist and locals say that it is one of the most authentic sports bar in the city. Visitors in groups come here to enjoy and socialize while watching a football, basketball or hockey game. The place is also decorated with autographed jerseys from professional players.

The bar is open from 7:30am till midnight. It serves breakfast, lunch and dinner. It has a wide array of drinks, from soft drinks to hard drinks.

The noise is usually low, but if there is a game, expect for some cheering around the bar.

More than a dozen of televisions are situated around the bar. There are even televisions in the restroom, so you do not miss anything from the game.

Prices: Drinks and foods start at $7. Selected food prices drop by 50% after 7:00pm.

How to get there from the National Mall: Make your way to 7th Street Northwest and walk towards the North. Turn left to Indiana Avenue and find the bar at the left side of the street.

Solly's Kostume Karaoke Bar

1942 11th St Northwest
+1 202-232-6590
Solly's Kostume Karaoke Bar
http://sollysbooking.wixsite.com/sollys
Solly's Kostume Karaoke Bar Map
https://goo.gl/maps/mEhCJ8hVARP2

You cannot leave Washington without visiting this bar. Many tourists end their vacation by visiting this bar, which is named as the best karaoke bar in Washington DC by top trip advising sites.

Many visitors come to the bar in costumes. As the night deepens, the bar becomes a big party with everyone cheering for anyone who sings, whether in tune or out of tune.

The bar is open from 3:00pm to 1:30am. They serve dinner but the menu is limited. However, they have a wide array of drinks.

Price: Prices starts at $4 for both foods and drinks.

How to get there from the National Mall: Take a bus heading to Fort Trotten at the stop in 12th Street and Constitution Avenue. Get off at the stop located in 11th Street and U Street. The bar is a few steps from there.

9

Top Five Cafes to Visit

A Baked Joint

440 K St NorthWest
+1 202-408-6985
A Baked Joint Website
www.abakedjoint.com
A Baked Joint Map
https://goo.gl/maps/qtj0gdkF1YE2

The café is a good place for light breakfast and brunch. It serves gourmet sandwiches and delicious baked goodies. Their breads are handmade and made in the traditional methods. The café is open from 7:00am to 3:00pm. They only serve dinner on weekends, where they close at 10:00pm.

The prices of drinks and foods range from $2 to $15.

How to get there from the National Mall: From the Smithsonian

Museum, walk to the bus stop in 10th Street and Pennsylvania Avenue. Ride the bus moving north to Rhode Island Avenue. Get off at K Street and walked a little further to find the café.

The Wydown Coffee Bar

1924 14th St Northwest
+1 202-507-8411
The Wydown Coffee Bar Website
www.thewydown.com
The Wydown Coffee Bar Map
https://goo.gl/maps/HRgrvr87Xn32

It is a traditional coffee bar that many tourists complimented as a coffee bar that can compete with Starbucks. It offers different varieties of non-alcoholic drinks. They also offer no-sugar or special diet drinks.

They offer sandwiches, cookies and cupcakes along with their drinks. The place is also elegantly designed. It is a very comfortable place to relax and read some books.

It opens from 6:30am to 9:00pm, but it only opens from Wednesday to Sunday. Prices of drinks and foods start at $4.

How to get there from the National Mall: Follow the direction to the Solly's bar as instructed in the previous section. Take a left and head to 14th Street. Go down south of 14th Street and you can find the café.

Three Fifty Bakery and Coffee Bar

1926 17th St Northwest
+1 202-629-1022
Three Fifty Bakery and Coffee Bar Website
www.threefifty.com
Three Fifty Bakery and Coffee Bar Map
https://goo.gl/maps/fR38TrhNDWF2

This small bakery offers a home-style baking experience. The baked goodies and breads are spread on a shelf and you can just pick it up or take a slice by yourself. The coffees and teas are also delicious and served elegantly.

The place is relaxing and quiet. The price is affordable and you can enjoy a lot with just $3.50.

The place operates from 7:00am to 7:00pm.

How to get there from the National Mall: Take a bus heading North to Silver Spring Station from the Constitution Avenue bus station. Stop at the 16th Street and U Street Station. Turn left at Hampshire Avenue and proceed to 17th Street.

Emissary Café

2032 P St Northwest
+1 202-748-5655
Emissary Café Website
http://www.emissarydc.com/
Emissary Café Website
https://goo.gl/maps/9036J9NevUw

The café is open only from Wednesday to Sunday. It opens at 7:00am, but the closing time varies each day, but it is usually 10:00pm. It offers breakfast, lunch and dinner. If your hotel is near the DuPont Circle, it is a good place to grab breakfast before starting your day around the city.

The prices of drinks start at $2.50 while food and pastry start at $4.
How to get there from the National Mall: Head to the Metro Center Station and board the Metrorail to the DuPont Circle Station. Head west

to Q Street and make a left on 20th Street until you reach P Street. Turn right and you will find the café.

The Potter's House

1658 Columbia Rd Northwest
+1 202-232-5483
The Potter's House Website
http://pottershousedc.org/
The Potter's House Map
https://goo.gl/maps/jAV8ve9KSB42

The café doubles as a book store and a library. You can buy some books and also rent some books. It is a popular meeting place for those who want to get creative ideas. It is also a good place to socialize with members of book clubs.

It only opens from Wednesday to Sunday from 8:00am to 8:00pm. Drinks start at $2 while food starts at $5.

How to get there from the National Mall: Ride the Greenbelt rail from the Penn Quarter Station to the Columbia Heights Station. Head South to 14th Street and Irving Street. Turn right to Columbia. The café is at the left side.

10

Top Five Museums to Visit

Smithsonian Museums

Constitution Avenue, NW
+1 202-633-1000

Smithsonian National Museum of American History Website
www.americanhistory.si.edu
Smithsonian National Museum of American History Map
https://goo.gl/maps/mFmyJasztLm

Smithsonian National Museum of Natural History Website
www.naturalhistory.si.edu
Smithsonian National Museum of Natural History Map
https://goo.gl/maps/SJEr8KVPSiz

Visiting these museums is a must for a tourist. It is one of the main sites in the National Mall. Entrances to both museums are free and it is open 364 days a year from 10:00am to 5:30pm.

The museums are huge and packed with many exhibits and educational materials. You can book a tour if you want to be guided as you explore the museums. If you are into History, Science, and Arts, you might end up using a whole day exploring these museums.

The National Gallery of Art

6th & Constitution Ave NW, Washington, DC 20565, USA
+1 202-737-4215
The National Gallery of Art

www.nga.gov Website
The National Gallery of Art Map
https://goo.gl/maps/oHLNvPAhYPP2

The National Gallery of Art is also composed of two buildings. It showcases American and European Arts from modern to post-modern eras. It is open from 10:00am to 5:00pm for 364 days. The entrance is also free.

Exhibits from new artists or art collectors are sometimes hosted in this museum, too.

It is also located in the National Mall and only a few miles from the US Capitol Building.

United States Holocaust Memorial Museum

100 Raoul Wallenberg Pl SW, Washington, DC 20024,USA
+1 202-488-0400
United States Holocaust Memorial Museum Website
https://www.ushmm.org/online/end-of-year/
United States Holocaust Memorial Museum Map
https://goo.gl/maps/XvnWztPDhJR2

The museum is a few meters away from the National Mall. It is a museum dedicated to learning about the tragic genocide committed against the Jews in World War I and to remember those who had survived the event. The museum presents the events in exhibits and by multi-media. You can also read or watch the testimonies of those who survived the holocaust.

It is open from 10:00am to 5:00pm every day except on Yum Kippur and Christmas day. During spring and summer, you would need to get a ticket before you can enter. The ticket is still free, but if you avail it online, it would cost $1. It is to avoid crowding during this season.

To get to the museum from the National Mall: From the National Museum of American History, head south via 14th Street. Take a right when you reach Independence Avenue. The museum would be visible at the right side of the road.

International Spy Museum

800 F St., Northwest
+1 202-393-7798
International Spy Museum Website
https://www.spymuseum.org/
International Spy Museum Map
https://goo.gl/maps/9yVmU7EcRyw

If you are a spy movie fan or a James Bond wannabe, you will enjoy this museum. It contains artifacts that international spies had used through the years. It also gives you an interactive experience on how to be a spy. Non-English speaker tourist may find it difficult to enjoy the interactive experience, but it is still worth a try.

The museum is open from 10:00am to 6:00pm. The fee is about $22 for those above 12 years old and $15 for those above 7 years old. Children below 7 years old are free. Discounts are given to senior citizens, retired military and war veterans.

To get to the museum from the National Mall: Follow Constitution Avenue until 9th Street. Turn left and head north until you reach F Street. Turn right to reach the Museum.

National Air and Space Museum

6th and Independence Ave., Southwest
+1 202-633-2214
National Air and Space Museum Website
https://airandspace.si.edu/
National Air and Space Museum Map
https://goo.gl/maps/sPpXhnQaF6P2

This museum shows how aircrafts and spaceships had develop over the years. You can see some of the oldest planes and rockets in America and all those that made a difference in the world.

It is a little far from Washington DC and not accessible to other public transport. You can easily access this museum from the Washington Dulles International Airport. Dulles buses leave every 20 minutes exclusively to this museum. It can be the first place you will visit or last place to visit during your vacation.

The museum entrance is free. It is open from 10:00am to 5:30pm.

11

Top Five Art Galleries to Explore

Smithsonian American Art Museum

F St NW & 8th St Northwest
+1 202-633-1000
Smithsonian American Art Museum Website
www.americanart.si.edu
Smithsonian American Art Museum Map
https://goo.gl/maps/RGLtEBcpYfC2

The museum is only across the International Spy Museum and beside the Capitol One Arena. It is home to old American paintings, portraits of the presidents and other artworks from famous and anonymous artists. It is a good stop after your spy experience and before a Wizard's game.

   The painting is open every day except on Christmas Day from 11:00am to 7:00pm. Entrance is free.

Renwick Art Gallery

1661 Pennsylvania Ave Northwest
+1 202-633-2850
Renwick Art Gallery Website
https://americanart.si.edu/visit/renwick

Renwick Art Gallery Map
https://goo.gl/maps/83wHsTbbw6s

The gallery is part of the Smithsonian American Art Museum. It showcases art exhibits from famous, upcoming and new American artists. It has an in-house store where you can buy handmade crafts, arts and souvenirs.

It is located at the right side of the White House. The gallery is open every day except on Christmas Day from 10:00am to 5:00pm. Entrance is still free.

Kreeger Museum

2401 Foxhall Rd Northwest
+1 202-337-3050
Kreeger Museum Website
www.kreegermuseum.org
Kreeger Museum Map
https://goo.gl/maps/7vwJ84ZGdaz

This museum used to be a residential building. It is smaller than most of the art galleries and has fewer collections. However, the collections are rare and can only be seen in this museum.

It is open from Tuesday to Saturday from 10:00am to 4:00pm. The entrance for adult is $10 and $8 for students and senior citizens. Children below 7 years old are free. Members are also free.

To get to the museum from the National Mall, board the bus heading west to Sibley Hospital from E Street and 13th Street. Get off between Greenwich and Foxhall Road. Head northwest until you reach the museum.

Hirshhorn Museum

Independence Ave Southwest
+1 202-633-1000
Hirshhorn Museum Website
https://hirshhorn.si.edu/
Hirshhorn Museum Map
https://goo.gl/maps/qQSet9mcyG72

This is another museum funded by the Smithsonian Institution and located in National Mall. It contains different kinds of arts, including multi-media and photography. It is famous for its collection of Garden Sculptures.

The museum opens at 10:00am and closes at 5:00pm. You can visit every day except Christmas Day. Admission is free.

Arthur M. Sackler Gallery

Independence Ave Southwest
+1 202-633-1000
Arthur M. Sackler Gallery Website
https://www.freersackler.si.edu/
Arthur M. Sackler Gallery Map
https://goo.gl/maps/xVg2WgkApwT2

The gallery is funded by the Smithsonian Institution. It is located in the National Mall. Admission is free.

The gallery features Asian art collections. You can see paintings, sculptures and artifacts from different Asian countries. Museum personnel are willing to explain some facts about the arts and how to operate some instruments featured in the museum.

The gallery is open from 10:00am to 5:30pm.

12

Landmarks to Visit

Lincoln Memorial Monument

2 Lincoln Memorial Cir NW, Washington, DC 20037,USA
+1 202-426-6841
Lincoln Memorial Circle Website
https://www.nps.gov/linc/index.htm
Lincoln Memorial Circle Map
https://goo.gl/maps/AAqCEa5NAYQ2

Built to honor the 16th US president, the statue serves as the landmark for the western end of the National Mall. A large statue of Abraham Lincoln greets the visitor in a Greek inspired building. In front of the memorial, you can explore the reflecting pool, which had been shown in many movies.

While you are in the premises, you can also visit the monuments for Franklin Roosevelt, Martin Luther King, Korean War Memorial and Vietnamese War Memorial.

The United States Capitol Building.

East Capitol St NE & First St SE, Washington, DC 20004, USA
+1 202-226-8000

The United States Capitol Building Website
https://www.visitthecapitol.gov/
The United States Capitol Building Map
https://goo.gl/maps/BWppaxoy7j72

Ending the National Mall in the east is the United States Capitol Building. It is considered to be one of the most important buildings in the world. It is the place where the Senate and the House of Representatives convene to create federal laws or even declare war.

It is not fully open to the public, but it has a visitor center, which is open every day from 10:00am to 4:30pm.

Library of Congress

101 Independence Ave Southeast
+1 202-707-5000

Library of Congress Website
www.loc.gov
Library of Congress Map
https://goo.gl/maps/f2VaZVyKoG12

It is the World's biggest library and contains about 16 million books from around the world. The library is also beautifully designed. You will enjoy reading books in their original versions or annotated versions. It is also kid-friendly and a nice place to enjoy a quiet time with your family.

The library is to the east from the US Capitol and across the US Supreme Court.

Georgetown University

3700 O St Northwest
+1 202-687-0100
Georgetown University Website
www.georgetown.edu
Georgetown University Map
https://goo.gl/maps/vhSabJshHrS2

Georgetown University is regarded as one of the Ivy League univer-sities in the world. Students from around the world attend this school to get the best education. Anyone can enter the gates of Georgetown University at any time. You can walk around the campus and admire the beautiful architectural designs of the building.

However, you cannot enter most of the buildings unless you are part of a tour. A student ID or personnel ID is required to enter some buildings, like the library and laboratories.

It is easier to reach the university from the DuPont Circle. Just head to the bus stop at P Street and 18th Street and board a bus heading west to Georgetown University. The bus will drop you at the gate near 37th Street and O Street.

The White House

1600 Pennsylvania Ave Northwest
+1 202-456-1111
The White House Website
www.whitehouse.gov
The White House Map
https://goo.gl/maps/4CZuxFQrFHz

Every tourist should visit and have a photo opportunity of the White House while in DC. It is regarded, arguably, as the home of the most powerful leader in the world. The White House is still beautiful even if you only see it from the outside.

Local tourists can enter the White House, if they acquired a recommen-dation from their congressman at least 90 days from the date of visit. International tourists may not have the same opportunity, but they can still enjoy the sight of the historic building. A visit during the holiday season is highly recommended.

13

Safety Tips When Travelling Around the City

Be cautious while you are travelling in the city. DC still has mobs roaming around the town. As a tourist, here are some things you need to remember to remain safe:

Keep your smartphone, cameras and other gadgets in your bag or pockets while in the bus stop or subway stations. The bus stop and subway stations are the favorite place of the mobs. They might grab your gadget while they are getting out of the bus or the train and you would be caught off guard.

Keep your personal belonging in check while traveling. Pickpockets and snatchers would take the opportunity of snatching your purse, phones, necklace and other personal belongings while you are taking pictures of the landmarks.

Always make sure to bring your ID and a machine copy of your passport. There are swindlers around the area that would accuse you of crimes, like sexual harassment or physical injuries, without any reason. Then, they would offer that you should settle instead. If this happens, you can easily go to a police station, present your ID and seek assistance as a tourist to deter the swindlers.

Watch out for those bikes. Speeding bikes are more dangerous than the cars in Washington DC. Do not wander mindlessly in bike lanes or you may be hit by locals that are speeding to get to their work or school.

14

Suggested Three-Day Itinerary

Time of Arrival: 12:00pm

Day 1

Check in from one of the hotels near DuPont Circle.

Have a hearty lunch from Emissary Café.

Head down to visit Georgetown University. It will take about 2 hours to travel and explore the University.

Head to the Exorcist Steps, the landmark featured in the movie "The Exorcist". You can take photos if you like.

Have some snacks from Georgetown Cupcake.

You can head to Georgetown Waterfront Park and enjoy the view of Potomac River at sunset. The park is just a block from the café.

After sunset, head to DuPont Circle and have dinner at Annie's Paramount Steakhouse.

Have some drinks at the Fox and Hounds Lounge and socialize before retiring for the night.

Day 2

Breakfast at Crimson Diner

Visit the International Spy Museum for two hours.

Visit the Smithsonian American Art Museum.

Visit the Crimson One Arena for photo opportunities.

Lunch at Old Ebbit Grill.

Visit Renwick Art Gallery.

From this point, rent a bicycle.

Explore the outsides of the White House.

Have the Monument tour. From Albert Einstein Memorial to Thomas Jefferson Memorial.

Go straight to US National Holocaust Museum.

Head back to Lincoln Monument and watch the sunset from the reflecting pool.

Visit Washington Memorial and bike around National Mall to admire the lighted buildings and landmarks.

Have dinner at Ambar Capitol Hills Restaurant. After dinner, bike along Naval Yard and take a visit at Nationals Park, home of the Washington Nationals baseball team.

Proceed to Pearl Street Warehouse to unwind and enjoy some live bands before retiring.

Day 3

Explore the museum at the Constitution Avenue side of National Mall. Allocate around one hour for each of the museum.

Have lunch at US Capitol Restaurant. Explore the Capitol grounds and tour around Library of Congress.

Take a tour of the museums in the Independence Avenue side of the National Mall. Allocate one hour for each museum.

Proceed to Rooftop Terrace Restaurant at Kennedy Center to have some dinner. Take a view of the National Mall from the rooftop.

Enjoy a performance at Kennedy Center.

If you have the budget, you can have a late dinner at Jack Rose Dining Salon, but save your budget for the drinks.

Head down to Solly's Kostume Karaoke and have fun with the locals and other tourists on your last night in the city.

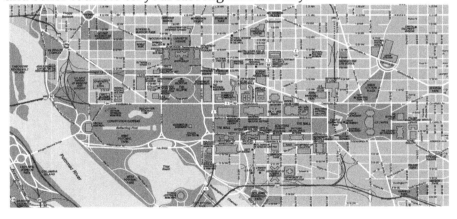

15

Conclusion

Thank you for downloading this book.

I hope that this book sparked your interest to spend some quality and memorable time in the historic city of Washington DC.

I hope that with this book, you can maximize your short 3-day vacation. The places included in this book are only the top recommendations. There are still more things that awaits you in DC.

Always keep safe on your travel and enjoy.

16

Thank You

I want to thank you for reading this book! I sincerely hope that you received value from it!

If you received value from this book, I want to ask you for a favour. Would you be kind enough to leave a review for this book on Amazon?

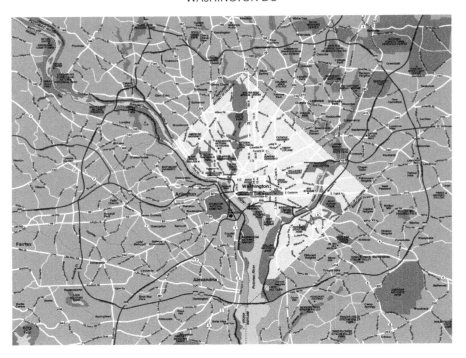

Made in the USA
Coppell, TX
06 June 2022

78523969R00057